# To Do As Adam Did
## Selected Poems
## of Ronald Johnson

# To Do As Adam Did:

## Selected Poems of

# Ronald Johnson

Edited by Peter O'Leary

Talisman House, Publishers
Jersey City, New Jersey

Published in the United States of America by
Talisman House, Publishers
P.O. Box 3157
Jersey City, New Jersey 07303-3157

Manufactured in the United Sates of America
Printed on acid-free paper

ISBN: 1-58498-004-4

The works selected for *To Do As Adam Did* were originally published in the following books: *A Line of Poetry, a Row of Trees* (The Jargon Society, 1964), *The Book of the Green Man* (Norton, 1967), *Valley of the Many-Colored Grasses* (Norton, 1969), *Songs of the Earth* (Grabhorn-Hoyem, 1970), *Eyes & Objects* (The Jargon Society, 1976), *RADI OS* (Sand Dollar, 1977), *ARK: The Foundations* (North Point Press, 1980), *ARK: 50* (Dutton, 1984), and *ARK* (Living Batch, 1996).

# CONTENTS

# from *The Different Musics* (1969)

# *Songs of the Earth* (1970)

# from *Eyes* & *Objects* (1976)

# from *RADI OS* (1977)

# from *ARK* (1996)

## from *The Shrubberies*
(previously unpublished)

# Peter O'Leary

## Quod Vides Scribe In Libro

"What thou seest, write in a book," trumpets the Voice of God to John the Revelator, newly exiled from Ephesos, occulted in a cave on a rocky upslope on the isle of Patmos. The Grotto of the Revelation, at the center of the Monastery of the Apocalypse, was designated nearly a thousand years ago. The ceiling of the cave is riven by a three-way cleft, signifying the Trinity; pilgrims can touch the ledge of rock where John leaned as he received his revelation; they can place their hands on the place where he rested his head as he saw the seven stars and the seven candles. The cave of the Grotto reminds us that vision is as real as stone. Likewise, the books that record such vision. Dante believed just as much: before he leaves the earthly paradise at the summit of Purgatorio to ascend in Beatrice's chariot to the heavenly Paradiso, she tells him: "for the sake of the world that lives in sickness, hold your eyes on the chariot, and what you see, be sure to write it when you return."

Ronald Johnson's poetry is visionary. Like Blake's poetry—and Blake was one of his heroes—it is at once expansive and minutely particular. In Johnson's poetry one finds the collapse of scale evident in Blake's phrase "all time takes place within the pulsation of an artery." It is visionary in that it is concerned with poetry as a mode of seeing—in a spiritual as well as a literal (optic) sense. Vision comes into play in Johnson's work through a variety of techniques. His poetry is a collage of quotations and observations: he quoted from Samuel Palmer or William Bartram just as easily as from the dictionary. "ARK 37" is made up entirely from quotations snipped from Roger Tory Peterson's *Field Guide to the Western Birds of North America*. Johnson was a concrete poet; he looked at letters and words as building blocks. His *Songs of the Earth*, contained here, shows us that even typography, through the alteration of a single letter, can be lyrical. By the time he wrote *ARK*, he could include in "BEAM 8" a line of poetry that reads: "()" to indicate the image of the curved surface of the eye looking outward; ")(" shows the same eyes looking inward. "BEAM 18" of *ARK* is Johnson's handprint; there is nothing more concrete than the word made flesh. To these, I would add Johnson's remarkable sense of the page: he has composed some of the most dazzling page displays in recent American poetry. The early poems in *A Line of Poetry, a Row of Trees* avail wild margins and long lines followed by very short lines. Eventually he discovered the centered justification that unifies *ARK* in a composition that is radial, bilateral, symmetrical.

Above all, Johnson knew that seeing and naming can be one and the same. For the visionary poet, as Johnson knew, the immediacy of experience takes precedent over received systems of thought or belief. All things must be named anew, and language and vision thus approach a horizon. I take the title for this collection from "BEAM 50" in *ARK*, which begins:

> "To do as Adam did"
> through the twilight's fluoride glare Mercury in perihelion
> (rotating exactly three times
> while circling the sun twice)
> to Pluto foot tilt up the slide at either plane
> and build a Garden of the brain.

What did Adam do? He named: naming built the Garden he dwelt in, allowing him to see it through words. Johnson recognizes the brain and the universe as mirror images: astrophysics is horticulture; scientific perception is gardening. Recently, I came upon the source of the opening quotation while reading Thomas Traherne, who wrote in his poem "The Apostasy,"

> All bliss
> Consists in this,
> To do as Adam did . . .

Johnson's poetry is nearly devoid of autobiography, confession, or the complaint that often accompanies these modes. Has there been a more blissful poet than Johnson? To read Johnson is to feel the pleasure of Adam naming things.

Johnson was however no Adamist, no poet in the wilderness. He spent his life first in Ashland, a small town in western Kansas flooded by the grasses of the prairie whose shores were Oz. He took a Bachelors degree from Columbia University, living in New York in the late fifties. He then wandered around Appalachia and Britain with Jonathan Williams for a number of years, staying the next twenty-five years in San Francisco before finally returning to Kansas where he died in 1998.[*] He formed his poetry with these places, and the people in these places, firmly in mind. Johnson's models in his art were his mentor

---

[*]For a fuller account of Johnson's life, see Eric Murphy Selinger's entry on Johnson in the *Dictionary of Literary Biography* (Detroit: Gale Research, Inc., 1996).

Jonathan Williams, as well as the Black Mountain poets—mainly Charles Olson and Robert Duncan; also, and especially, Louis Zukofsky, and William Carlos Williams, along with Ezra Pound. His models for his style of visionary poetry were Whitman, Blake, Wordsworth, Christopher Smart, George Herbert, and Dante. He was also keenly influenced by so-called naive artists, including Simon Rodia, builder of the Watts Towers, the Facteur Cheval, who built the Ideal Palace in Hauterives, and Raymond Isidore, who devised the mosaic house at Chartres. This last group points to the other overwhelming quality of Johnson's work: besides its visionary qualities, it is architectonic. Johnson's father owned a lumberyard in Ashland, Kansas. Some of the poet's earliest memories were of hiding among the piles of wood under the prairie sky. The only other poet whose work compares to Johnson's in this respect is that of Ian Hamilton Finlay, a mainstay in the concrete poetry movement. Where Finlay has made a literal garden out of the words of his poetry, in the form of sundials, monuments, sculptures, and quotations carved in marble, Johnson showed that the act of collecting, arranging, and caring for words was itself an act of gardening. Words are flowers, leaves, trees. Johnson saw poetry as a kind of cultivation, as the careful imposition of the gardener on the natural growth of the world.

A few words about this selection. I have gathered work that represents the span of Johnson's career. To read all of his work chronologically is to be impressed by the high quality of the work throughout. In whichever mode he was writing, whether the Olsonian projective mode of the early poems, the concision of the concrete poems, or the invented forms of *ARK*, Johnson's poems consistently bristle with interest. Nonetheless, *ARK* was Johnson's magnum opus. In the end, Johnson's reputation and legacy stands or falls with *ARK*. It took him twenty years to write; he conceived it as a "big" poem to take its place beside *The Cantos*, *"A"*, and *The Maximus Poems*. It is an intensely integral poem; one of the incredible pleasures of reading it is to experience how the poem reveals itself to its readers and instructs them how to read it, page after page, section after section. Fortunately, the poem is essentially plastic and does not seem meaningless in excerpt. Since *ARK* is Johnson's great work, it seemed futile not to include as much of it as possible. For this reason, nearly a third of this selection comes from *ARK*.

I have clustered my choices for this selection around four Adamic notions in Johnson's work: 1) The Garden & the Gardener; 2) Orpheus; 3) Thoreau; 4) the Prairie. Each of these serves less as a topic than as an organizing theme in the poetry. Most of the selections from *A Line of Poetry, a Row of Trees* (The

Jargon Society, 1964) first appeared in a special issue of *Poetry* magazine on the "Long Poem." This issue featured the work of Olson, Duncan, Zukofsky, Robert Lowell, John Berryman, and Gary Snyder. This was Johnson's first appearance in print. *The Book of the Green Man* (Norton, 1967) was Johnson's journal poem from the year he spent walking through England with Jonathan Williams. Toward the end of his life, Johnson realized that it was written and published at the same time as Basil Bunting's *Briggflatts*, a poem he very much admired; he relished the coincidence that both were long seasonal poems about the English countryside. "The Different Musics" and "The Unfoldings" first appeared in *Valley of the Many-Colored Grasses* (Norton, 1969), which collected an edited version of A *Line of Poetry, a Row of Trees* with new work. Both of these poems are important in the way they anticipate the technical and visionary aspects of *ARK*.

Songs of the Earth was one of Johnson's contributions to the concrete poetry movement. These visual settings of Mahler's piece of music were originally published by the Grabhorn-Hoyem Press in 1970 in an extremely limited edition. Johnson once remarked to me that this was his favorite book of his own poetry. He thought of it as nearly perfect. *Eyes & Objects*, originally published by the Jargon Society in 1976, was printed as a catalogue to an exhibition. Its cover features a visionary portrait of Johnson, blurred into an essence, by Ralph Eugene Meatyard. In this book, Johnson shapes words as sculpture. This includes, as in "World-Framed Page," the molecules of the page itself as a shapeliness with which language interacts. *RADI OS*, published by the Sand Dollar Press in 1977, is one of Johnson's most popular poems. This rewriting of Milton's *Paradise Lost* is nearly unexcerptable, but a morsel of it seemed necessary if only to show what the poet was able to see in Milton's poem.

Two of the selections from *ARK* deserve special mention: "BEAMS 21, 22, 25, *The Song of Orpheus*" is one of the tours de force of the poem. It opens with a quotation from the beginning of *RADI OS*. This is quickly followed by "PALMS," a reading through *The Book of Psalms* in which Johnson selected, in order, at least one word from each Psalm to construct his own poem. Not an aleatory method, Johnson's selective reading—much like what he accomplished in *RADI OS*—is an essential act of vision, seeing what words live in the text already, and then drawing them out. Johnson once said to me that "BEAM 30, The Garden" is the centerpiece of *ARK*, a vision not of Eden itself but of what is done there. By including this here, I can correct a typesetter's mistake that appears in both previous published versions of this poem: the line "This is the body of light" is to be followed by the remaining page blank. Light, Johnson shows, flows from the page.

"The Shrubberies" are Johnson's last poems, written over the course of the last five years of his life. When he moved back to Kansas, he took a job, eventually, as a gardener and handyman at an historic mansion and park in Topeka. Having already recorded his grand vision in the book *ARK*, his eyes were once again attracted by minutiae. These poems record passing events and time. To this brief selection of "Shrubs," as he called them, I have added the very last poem Johnson wrote.

May 24, 1999
Chicago

ACKNOWLEDGEMENTS: I would like to thank Guy Davenport, Joseph Donahue, Joel Felix, Ed Foster, Devin Johnston, Michael O'Leary, Jodi Panula, Jed Rasula, Eliot Weinberger, and David Wilk. My gratitude for help & encouragement in putting this collection together.

from *A Line of Poetry, A Row of Trees* (1964)

# SHAKE, QUOTH THE DOVE HOUSE

'A laurustine bear in blossom
with a juniper hunter in berries,
a lavender pig with sage growing in his belly
& a pair of maidenheads in fir, in great
forwardness'.

        This is the Garden, where all is a poet's
        topiary. Where even the trees
        shall have tongues, green aviaries,
        to rustle at his will.

        And as I sit here, my pipe
        alight, coos like a turtle-dove in the wood—

        its smoke a live-oak, in still air.

Where
the smokes curl up, the moss hangs down:
let us call it Arden

& live in it!

    For the poet
    'may draw into his Description
all the Beauties of the Spring & Autumn, & make
the whole year contribute
something to render it the more agreeable.
His Rose-Trees, Wood-bines & Jessamines may flower together,
& his beds be cover'd
at the same time
with Lilies, Violets & Amaranths.
His Soil is not restrained to any Set of Plants, but
is proper
either fort Oaks or Myrtles,
& Oranges may grow

        wild in it'.

It is here—
(the growing walls
a ceiling green

above me)
I have made clear space

to cultivate

the Wild, Espaliered, Tangled,
Clipped

estate. Here—

both lines of poetry, rows
of trees,
shall spring all

seasons
out 'of the lust of

the earth,
without
a formal seed'.

And the doves, overnight, will rise
as a *fumus*

*terrae:*
inhabitants of air
& undergrowth

alike.

# SAMUEL PALMER: THE CHARACTERS OF FIRE

> In the road above me, I was struck with the peculiar appearance of a very white shining cloud, that lay remarkably close to the ground. The sun was nearly setting, but shone extremely bright. I walked up to the cloud, & my shadow was projected into it; when a very unexpected, & beautiful scene was presented to my view. The head of my shadow was surrounded at some distance by a circle of various colours, whose centre appeared to be near the situation of the eye. . . .
>
> JOHN HAYGARTH, 1790

As if the flashing of mackerel in phosphorescent sea,
the eye, a swimmer,
covered with fire after every immersion
in the air,
      is to Palmer

to be led beyond
the horizon, to where—as a hand makes sheaves—
it gathers to itself all light

in visionary harvest:

        a *situation* of
        the eye,

        that to Coleridge, the Marigold,
        Monk's-hood,
        Orange-lily & Indian pink
        flash with light—

        or that Darwin observe phosphorus in eyes
        of a horse,

           & water-drops which lie

         like quicksilver on cabbages.


I walked up to the cloud,

'a country
where there is no
night'

but of moons
& with beads of fish

in the furrow,

& on each
ear, beneath a husk
of twilight

were as many suns as
kernels,
& fields were far

as the eye
could reach.

Then dipping their silver oars,

the eyes
shed characters of fire
in the grain,

its sheaves as if mackerel
shone on the waves
of air.

# Four Orphic Poems

*for Elizabeth Sewell*

I

'Sentences uttered

with your back to a wall',
clear
as nails


but with all a lichen's curious thrust.

The wall is one
of bone,

made by a forehead:

behind it, Bread, Fire & Writing came, of that greening-purple cabbage
(that is the brain)


glistening in its field in the first dews of morning.


Outside,
between bone & page, circlings

of sap, stars, tide


hold meaning
as a nest holds speckled bird's eggs,

& I (like
Thoreau) sit here engrossed,

'between a microscopic & a telescopic
world',
attempting to read

the twigged, branchy writing

of frost, spider & galactic cluster. That the syllables!

—rock & flower & animal
alike—
among the words,


make Order.


The field is newly plowed & unfenced. Its furrows

hold innumerable seeds
which have come on the wind, on wings
of birds.

What new green
script

will crack their burr & prickle? What words

must I corner like
hedge-hogs


to put them on a page?

## II

There is an exquisite movement, like it were chaos,

but of a sweet proportion
& order:
the atoms, cells & parsley-ferns

of the universe.

Thus to Bacon it is 'not of much use
to recount
the exact varieties of flower,

shells, dogs, hawks',

& Palmer could make the trunk of a tree
like a mule's knee—

& a book in which there are thirty-three moons & vast flaming suns

'but never a cast shadow',

& Whitman
could make lines that were irregular as waves

of the Atlantic.

Halcyon, upon transformation after
transformation—

those 'hefts
of the moving world'
felt

underfoot:

we hurtle, rotate, disintegrate, re-form,
with every step.

# III

At night in the New Jersey woods, we were awakened
by the bucks
circling our camp.

They would stamp the earth
& cough

in their rut, continuing the night through.

They would pause only
at the beam of
a flashlight. Then rings of blue

orbs

burned back at us. Lyres,

remember,
were tuned to those intervals between the known
planets—Saturn, Jupiter, Mars,

Venus & Mercury—

to indicate the 'harmony', *music of the spheres,* that played

in a measure
hidden, ineluctable

to an ear.

'The eye is the first circle—
& the horizon which it forms is the second'.

These are instances,
signs:
the ring, the crown, the wreath, the blood-red eclipse

of suns,
the New Moon with the Old

in her arms,


& subtler harmonies, coming of growth
& of death.

In *Splendor Solis*, the sun rising over a cold, winter landscape:


a symbol of rebirth,
*coagulatio.*
The black rays of sun setting

within the earth:

a humid, marshy landscape, in the first warmth
of spring—

*putrefactio* & decay.


All night
the earth reverberating
with their hooves,

& at morning

the birds singing.

# IV

Nebula, whirlpool, mist & cloud; knotted, asymmetrical branchings

formed like a labyrinth

—are form, even as a sphere, crystal
& flower.

'Patterns

are temporary boundaries', the moving countries

where nothing
is seen in isolation.

*And Orpheus, the metamorphosis*

*before us*

of coral,
acanthus,

leopard's-paw, bird's-foot,

'sinuosities

of meadow'
& of rock as it moves

quietly

beneath lichen.

For 'where the figure is, the answer is'.

Newton
—it is said—did not show the cause of an apple falling,

only the similitude between the apple

& the stars.

# SUNFLOWERS

The sky is apple-green.
             A sower casts his seed
       in a dark field,
             while the sun, become pale as silver,
         encircles
             his head.


             After a day of hot sunshine,
there may radiate from the center
             along the petal,
         coruscations
             of light:
   'these shimmering blue vapors
             of an extreme
       tenuity'.


       There are those
             instances: Blake,
         Van Gogh—
             & even Stead's, as it stands alone,
       as 'tall as the pine'
             in a plain—
   like Cockscomb, Saffron-cup,
             that are light become
         vegetable.
             Or—
   like the mirror
             we make the sun—
round-cheeked, with hair of fire.
             This is the ornamental flower
     whose red florets spiral
             to the rays
         & ripen
             so heavy in the head, with
       seed,

stems
must be propped.


But the common Kansas
sunflower—
*Helianthus,*
is a composite so prolific
it has species
without name—
small,
speckled & pungent,
it will cover whole fields
in summer.
Among mullein, thistle, milkweed
hull,
as a 'murmuration'
of starlings—
swarmings
of bees:
it wheels like
skies of a shaggy, & many-headed,
sun.

# INDIAN CORN

Columbus, as the first Western eyes, called it
panic grass—Maize, of a 'quaking' ancestry, i.e., the
attempt, always, at classification. Though the myth of an Indian
*Chicomecoatl,* or an ear of blue kernel
shook out of the wings of a turkey (as it flew from
The-Star-That-Spreads-Its-Hair in a morning
sky), or *Kan* of the Codex, is a confusion of deities, closer,
as myth is, to roots: a confusion
of silk & of tassle, kept, in planting every row,
to assure that a characteristic
abundance of blues, reds, purples & yellows continue—in colors
that are pure, or striped,
or speckled as the egg of a turkey.


At the time of a new moon—
(for as the moon
grows, so will the corn)

when the leaves of the white-oak
are large
as a squirrel's foot,

the women (for the corn is a woman)
dance
& shake their hair loose

over their shoulders.
Flutes are played, so the earth
will loosen

for the kernel—
& when the sun rises
to meet the star of morning,

each
is stamped into an earth, ready
to receive it.

I remember once, as black clouds
gathered in the sky, I took
refuge from the sudden autumn shower
under a shock of corn,
& the smell damp earth made—
under it, in a sheltering
hollow, among the crisp, yellow stalks
—clings even now,
even as the mud that caked
on my boots, as I returned home.

What is myth, but the power to tell
the truth of it? In words
not even the *real* planted here—
with its rootlets reaching from the base
arrested in a movement down,
or its bright green
of leaves, caught in transpiration—
could tell. For truth
includes not only the even row
of kernels, but grey-black
growths, that I have seen split
the greenest husk


—& *Kan:*
in which scholars
cannot see the simplicity of a kernel

germinating:
feet curled above her head,
one hand holding the symbol of corn, & the other sprouting

as seeds below ground:
the triple root
as it grows down, & the one shoot curling up

to become a stalk—
& the moon, laid like a turkey egg
on a hill.

18

# QUIVERA

## I

Also reputed to be golden, Quivira:


Cibola, unknown
to Coronado, meant 'buffalo'

to the Indians, but onward, to El Dorado, 'The Gilded One',


a country where
boats were incrusted with gold, where
golden bells hung from trees


(though the food there,

said to be served on gold,


was buffalo).


'We took the hump from both sides of the hump
ribs, of all the carcasses. In taking out the hump
we inserted the knife at the coupling of the loin,
cutting forward down the lower side, as far
forward as the perpendicular ribs ran; then,
starting at the loin again, would cut down the
upper side, thus taking out a strip from a full-
grown animal about three feet long. Near the front
of the hump ribs it would be ten or twelve inches
wide & four or five inches thick. When first taken
out it was hung up for a couple of days with the

big end down. It became shrunken, tender &
brittle, with no taint. The front end had a streak of
lean alternating with fat & when fried in tallow,
made a feast for the gods'.


      The prairie soil was 'black & fat' &,

      according to Castaneda, the marrow of the land.


On that soil, later to be stripped
for prairie sod-houses,

wild turkeys
flocked among the persimmons

their flesh succulent from golden sand plums,
bitter

with china-berries.
The coyotes,

their eyes aglow on the dark horizon, barked at a moon
above the lowing

of buffalo, heard twenty miles
away.

And cottonwood trees, from whose buds
the Indians

made clear yellow, scattered their drift in spring
filling the gullies.


      The Quivirans
      were to tell Coronado

'the things
where you are now

are of great importance'.

## II

As Coronado turned to retrace his steps,
the Smoky Hills were visible north across a stream
enveloped in an atmospheric haze
in which the hills
became distant, impossible mountains—

'where you are now'

the Indians had said, 'of great

importance'.


The country they traveled over
was so level,
if one looked at the buffalo

the sky could be seen between their legs,

so that at a distance they appeared
to be smooth-trunked pines whose tops jointed—

& if there was
one bull, it seemed four
pines.

The country was round, as if
a man should imagine himself in a bowl, & could see sky
at its edge

an arrow's shot away.

And if any man
were to lie down on his back, he lost

sight
of the ground.

Did Coronado see also in that late summer storm,
before he turned south,
an horizon of dark funnels tapering
toward the earth, coming with the thunderous sound of a buffalo herd
out of the plains—a calm & sulphurous air
in which clouds were drawn like lightning toward the funnels—
scattering his men
to hide among grassy hollows?


A tornado against the sky
like buffalo

who were bearded as
goats,

with the hump of a camel, the mane
of a lion

& who carried
their tails erect as they ran,

like any European
scorpion.

O Coronado, all country
is round to

those who lose sight of the
ground.

Canceas, Cansez, Kansies, Konza: the Indian word

meaning smoky,

from an atmospheric condition

in the fall of the year, called

Indian Summer:

smoke in the air,

in Quivira.

# Lilacs, Portals, Evocations

Kansas, of
sand plums & muddy rivers
from where I come

where,
> once all roads led out, east, west,
> into high
> ways & winding sea roads,

> > where Zukofsky


up from Willow, Brooklyn Heights,
the streets of Gloucester out to Olson, Fort Point,
Ruggles at the Cut-Leaf Maples
Motel, Vermont,

& Ives under Danbury's
Maples,

> are now ways homeward.


'And where are you,
Mr. Johnson'?

> > quoth the Matron, & I
> > 'I am, madame,

> > here', I said, though it were much too simple

> > a conviction for her,

> > > O,

> > what to say
> > to 'what do you do'

'where are you going & where

do you come from'?

That neither were we

prepared for Rutherford?
how factories & filling stations, a winter day,

did not give way
to summer tree-lined streets
& dusk among porches,

how then we took

yellow tulips from a florist shop
toW.C.W.


—bulbs from other earth

than poetry's.


That I first played Ruggles
expecting Lilacs,
Portals, Evocations

of Whitman's lilacs?


the Kansas lilacs
brought fifty years before
'back east'

from lawns of Indiana, Kentucky,


eighty years before?

the lilacs we played inside, they were so large—
great prairie castles, of hidden doors
& windows only outward—

an odor, all
of America's springs,

lilacs?

If there are lyrics
grow in clusters, not 'melodies

of five octaves
apart'
      we cannot prepare

our ear for,

      I do not hear them here,

where no hedgerows,
but billboards, & even they lost in wheatfields,

in transit, always westward wherever we are,

from where I come.

from *The Book of the Green Man* (1967)

# The Oak of the Maze

Lichen.

Lion's shin, oak-limb, tomb:
all acquire
a hundred years'

skin,
a winter's pelt—bones

that 'being
striken one against
another

break out
like fire

& wax greene'.


Mistletoe. Its seeds
ripened
within birds—

out of the quickening gut,
it clings to oak.

An aerial
green,

white-berried.


Ivy. Springs out
of earth,
to cover it

with dark, shining leaves.

It is the mythic coat
of an oak—

made of a shining
& dark-
leaved thunder,

lightnings
& the owls

of its hollows.


There are connections in these

—between an earth, sentient with moles,
& the owl's
radiant eyes—

fine as a web drawn
by spiders,

close as the grain of oak . . .


from earth, to mistletoe, ivy & lichen, to owl's-
wing, to thunder, to lightning, to earth—& back.


There are many ways

to look at an oak, & one, with its
own eyes:

the blunt, burning push
of acorns

in an earth full

of movements, slight rustlings, as a passage of night-birds,
& bones

that 'being striken one against another

break out like fire

& wax greene'.

# EMANATIONS

'I am a walking fire, I am all leaves.'

'I find I incorporate gneiss, coal, long-threaded moss,
fruits, grains, esculent roots.
And am stucco'd with quadrupeds & birds all over'.


I find I advance with
sidereal motions
—my eyes containing substance

of the sun,
my ears built of beaks & feathers—

I ascend with saps

& flower in season

& eddy with tides.


With every moon,
I come from the darkness into incandescence.

My tongue assumes the apple's flesh
& my skin, the infinite spheres of the thistle's prickle. And as I
breathe

the wind has its billow—& all the grasses—


in a combing, mazy movement.

# April 13th

Here, the river swept great
curves
along wide valleys.

We left our footprints

green, behind,
as we followed the straight bright dew-path, meadow banks gleaming.


Clouds moved down the valley—their shadows
a river of huge dapples—their glowing masses opening above
as we came,

a white, enveloping progression.


Mid-day, whole
clouds lowered

& one leaned into wind to walk—
a brisk,
wet fog blowing—


though by evening the sun set westward
in our eyes

among slow cumulus that shafted bands of yellow
light


& remained black spaces
neither earth,
nor air,

suspended in that 'vacant interlunar cave'

where all the stars

revolved, wheeled, glittered.

# Upon First Opening a Cuckoo

I saw the sweet-briar & bon-fire & strawberry wire now

relaxed into intricate thicket.

It was as if seen in strong sunlight, flat

& tapestried, all edge & definition. Here, an airy bone shaped

like a plowshare, there, vibratory membranes within a space

from which the song must come: a *syrinx* (hollow

pipes of reeds) now silent

in return to the 'Salliter' of earth.

*Little more than*

*a drift of air, brought*

*into form by plumes.*

Mulch to stone.

Yeast of the clouds.

# WHAT THE EARTH TOLD ME

No surface is allowed to be bare,

& nothing to stand still. A man could forever study a pebble

& at last see dilations & expansions of the hills—

to pull the most slender stalk, is to jostle the stars,

& between the bearded grass

& man 'looking in the vegetable glass

of Nature', is a network of roots & suckers

fine as hairs.

*I threw a stone upon a pond*

& it bounded the surface, its circles interlacing

& radiating out to the most ephemeral edge.

Flint & Mica, Lichened Limestone, Shale & Sarcens, Sandstone, Soil.

*I saw the wind moving on a meadow*
& the meadows moving under wind—
lifting,  settling  &  accumulating.

Flint & Mica. Lichened Limestone,

Shale & Sarcens, Sandstone, Soil.

# WHAT THE AIR TOLD ME

It is breathed into Orpheus' lyre & as rocks & trees & beasts

is divided there. Its original strain


precedes the sound, by as much as echoes follow after:

the quivering of 'cow-quake', a 'loud audible

humming of bees on the down', stresses within the sustaining earth,

clouds of *fleece & mare's tail.*


I saw with single eye, the facet of the fly—

the infinitesimal mechanics & all the metallic sheens

of a blue-bottle. In a land where the sun grows fat on cloud

& *summer hasn't come*

*till your foot can cover twenty daisies,*


she came to the dark, open beak

& laid a myriad of eggs. And in two day's time the dead

bird's body simulated life: maggots in eye-socket &

under feather, in a subtle movement.


The White & The Glistening.

# WHAT THE LEAF TOLD ME

*Today I saw the word written on the poplar leaves.*

*It was* 'dazzle'. *The dazzle of the poplars.*


As a leaf startles out

from an undifferentiated mass of foliage,

so the word did from a leaf—

A Mirage Of The Delicate Polyglot

inventing itself as cipher. But this, in shifts & gyrations,

grew in brightness, so bright

the massy poplars soon outshone the sun . . .

'My light—my dew—my breeze—my bloom'. Reflections


In A Wren's Eye.

# WHAT THE LIGHT TOLD ME

It is now a circle, now a spiral or wheel.

It merges with the eye, with a wing or a sickle-shaped horn.

It takes on the form of beasts—a dragon, fish or bird.

As an orb, at summer solstice,
it balances on the altar-stone at Stonehenge—

& as beam, expands, elongates, twists & 'attenuates
itself into leafen gold
as a covering for the quince'.


With arc & parabolic
& serpent-oblique—'musical in ocular
harmony'. Expanding, elongating, twisting
& attenuating.


An encompassing eye.
*Within and out, round as a ball—*
*With hither and thither, as straight as a line.*
Slight as a fox-whisker,
spiraled, twined—rayed as chicory-flower.


*Within and out, round as a ball—*
*With hither and thither, as straight as a line.*
*With lily, germander*
*And sops-in-wine. With sweet-briar and*
*Bon-fire and strawberry wire*
*And columbine.*

A chryselephantine sky. The round earth
on flat paper. 'The clouds which drop fatness
upon our fields & pastures'.

Island—*eye-lands*—& piled mountains
of light. A circumambient voyage into the visible.

I saw that at Shoreham.


I saw hybernacula move
like clouds, & the turtle's eyes red
within.

I saw a badger root among soft
yellow plums of moonlight, & at dawn, a sheep
shake the dews
from its coat, in coronae.

I saw 'vegetable gold'
—the light of suns fold in upon itself,
as leaves
of a cabbage—

I watched the elder grow first
green, then white,
then a lustrous black.


'Thoughts on RISING
MOON with raving-mad splendour
of orange twilight glow on
landscape. I saw that at Shoreham'.

Shoreham—the ripeness
—proliferation. 'Excess more abundantly
excessive'. Its whale-shaped
hills, above the valleys of the hops
& apples. Its shepherds of the many-colored sheep.

I saw ascensions, transformations
& flights 'from a leaf
of kale, across the disc of a planet'.

I saw a world of Leviathan
& the thousand repetitions of spore & insect
intermixed.


Shoreham. Autumnal, mercurial.
A world where the skies
dome above, almost so high as to hold
both rising, meridian & setting suns, with moons large
as barn doors.

A land, perpetually coming
to harvest. The light come out of earth,
a heavy hay—& piled up in stooks
beneath the budding, leafing, flowering chestnut.
I saw that at Shoreham.


I saw all that at Shoreham
& more—the 'cherub-turtles'—the *Shining*

*Ones, where they commonly walk . . .*

## OF CERTAINE WHITE NIGHTS WHEREIN THE DARKES DOE SEEM TO GETTE UP & WALK & HOW WEE SAW DIVERS WONDERS IN BOTHE EARTH & ELEMENT.

As we descended to this valley,
where Samuel Palmer had used to walk—bareheaded
under the moon—
the passing clouds above
'did marvellously supple the ground'.

And there were seen many blackbirds to settle
as shapes of water on the land.


Out of the warm hills at our backs
a nebulous lightning
pulsed & flickered, a false
Aurora Borealis, enfolding us as we came.


*Wee had observed*
*these glows to collect as solid*
*as stones, at the sides of our eies—*

*& the hollows,*
*each, to appear to rise out*
*of its owne darkeness.*


We also came upon one tree,
out of those that abound here, whose leaves
seemed brought into curious relief
by the twilight being reflected upon one
side, & a waxing moon,
on the other—

*it is thus our nights, everywhere,*
*continued*
*but dusks of daies.*

*I walked up to the CLOUD,*

*'a country*
*where there is no*
*night'*

*but of moons*
*& with heads of fish*

*in the furrow,*

*& on each*
*ear, beneath a husk*
*of twilight*

*were as many suns as*
*kernels,*

*& fields were far*

*as the eye*
*could reach.*

*Then dipping their silver oars,*

*the eyes*
*shed characters of fire*
*in the grain,*

*its sheaves as if mackerel*
*shone on the waves*

*of air.*


*I walked up to the CLOUD*

*& the white light*
*opened*
*like flowers—*

*dog violet,*
*& asphodel, celandine,*

*red clover.*


*I walked up to the CLOUD*

*& peal after peal*
*rang out of earth.*

*First, stones*
*underfoot*
*in a sound like muffled*

*sheep-bells.*
*Then the roots of the trees*

*clanged:*
*rooks, rooks, blackbirds. Cuckoos awoke*
*in the tubers*

*—earth-worm & mole & turtle—*

*all danced to the thunder,*
*the peal & thunder.*

*A bellow & clamor*
*came out*
*of the hills:*

*in diapason—a dissonance*
*& musical order.*


ROOKS, ROOKS, BLACK-
BIRDS, CUCKOOS.

EARTH-WORM & MOLE
& TURTLE.

from *The Different Musics* (1969)

# THE DIFFERENT MUSICS

*for Robert Duncan*

come simultaneously
across water,
accumulating fume, spray, the flex of ripple.

As fume, from the Latin *fumus,* Greek
*thymos:* spirit, mind. "See

DUST, THEISM: cf.
FEBRUARY, FURY, PERFUME, THYME".


(Cf. means 'compare' &
'leads to useful, interesting, or related material that is not,
however, essential to an understanding of the meaning'.)


I find among DUST
vapor, storm, breath, smoke:

'the earthy remains of bodies once alive—
a confusion—
a single particle, as of earth'.

And THEISM out of *theos,* including breath & spirit
with demon, incubus—*bestia*:

beasts—& smokes.

FEBRUARY, Feast of Purification,
a month smoke rose from altars. Next

FURY (wrath, ire, turbulence
& madness)
the hectic *Furies*

& PERFUME, also a smoke,
a pungence—as in

THYME.


'An apparent confusion if lived with long enough
may become orderly'. Charles Ives

. . . accumulating,

a humus! (The upper strata—dry, newly-
fallen leaves, twigs, lichen.
Seeds from the size of the whiskered dandelion, to acorns
big as thumbs. Battalions of ants
& small moths imitating leaves & beetles & anonymous
bugs imitating pebbles.
A middle stratum of Sprouting
—blanched root-threads downward in a rich, dark
mold & cotyledons curling faintly green toward light—Sprouting
& Decay. Odors of rotted leaves—
deep reds, mahoganies &
ochre. Mauve froths, a bulbous fungus.
Bleached, lacy suckers studded in bits of glistening
quartz, or imbedded
among crushed, metallic wing-cases
of beetles.

And the under-ooze & loose loam of slug & worm.)

Sibelius                                          '. . . at dusk, when soft, strange
                                                      ventriloquisms come


in the country
heard                                           from holes in the ground . . .'
                                                      a polysyllabic,

overtones from a rye-
                                                      articulate echo

field


52

as he dozed
at the field's

edge.

A cow lows,

& the vibrant whorl

swirls!


Sounds come
to the ear,

transformed: pulling themselves up

by the boot-straps:

as if a new critter

altogether,
created

out of the marvellous canaries

of the air.

This exquisite & unending cacophony, sweet

roar upon roar

swelling, out of the silent
shell.

. . . ululations out of

multitudinous pores

each, a small voice, *slightly out of tune,*

rejoicing

in earth.

I put my ear to
the ground, & heard

the blood
rush to my head

thundering where the roots

drummed

& whispered as they grew: new
delicacies, new

tangle.

And the blood whispered *new delicacies, new*

*tangle.*

New extremities, new labyrinth
& branching, new, inextricable windings.

A new foliage of sensings:
sings & sings. . .

From here I hear the king-fisher's rattle,
a cardinal's
*whoitwhoitwhoitwhoitwhoitwhoit,*
the reiteration of a red-eyed vireo,
wren & thrasher, thrush—
the wood-thrush pushing its err-o-lay through the dusk—
*err-o-lay-ro-lay-ro*
—*pee-wee, pee-ur-wee, pee-wee*—
thin scissorings of black & white warblers, & whistling robins,
a chickadee,
titmouse & piping towhee,

messages of the air

(as the air assumes tongues in its swift passage)

wreathing in sibilant expansions

outward.


And night comes opening its arms like smokes to enfold us:
THE DANCERS!
Where their feet touch the earth
an encircling of plume, diaphanous featherings.
THE DANCERS!

And the dark came
—a ring of beasts, with smoldering eye—
to the edge of a grove,

its bearded & hoary branches sonorous to an inner wind
—err-o-lay-ro-lay-ro—
(a voice of the thrush from other throats)

THE DANCE! THE DANCING OUTWARD!

A spreading effulgence!
A resplendent 'hood' of light!
A choric turbulence, to which the worlds keep time.

Where their feet struck upon the earth
a pungence sprang up: strewings of thyme & of lavender.

And always the full-winged nights advance:
a field of robins erect
their red breasts facing east, into the rising sun.
OUTWARD!

FIRE IN FIRE, A DANCING FLAME, REDOUBLED LIGHT.

```
*   *   *   *   *   *   *

*   *   *   *   *   *   *

*   *   *   *   *   *   *

*   *   *   *   *   *   *

*   *   *   *   *   *   *

*   *   *   *   *   *   *

*   *   *   *   *   *   *

*   *   *   *   *   *   *

*   *   *   *   *   *   *

*   *   *   *   *   *   *
```

# The Unfoldings

This is the buoyant meadow, a bottomless

wave of fox-fire. A rustling 'rye' of stars, rooting,
downward, endlessly,

while its fires aspire upward, & its interstellar crickets pulse:

*Outward! Light! Inward! Darkness!*


Where once the world stood
surrounded,
on a cylindrical column, by a spherical bark

leaking fire—or

was circular, sublunary, wrapped in

a celestial crystalline onion-skin.


\*   \*   \*


Leeuwenhoek

went over that water, which, in winter
was very clear, but in 'the midst

of summer grew whitish
& there were then small green clouds permeating it'.

And he found in it
the slow
ovals of animals

moving

'pellucid', 'green & very shining'.

*     *     *

The ripe sparkling weeds wet us to the waist

as we walked
into the rising sun, 'oriented'
eastward

—conjuring us, the gold
intruders, out of congeries of pollen—

beckoned by pungencies, a multitude of spider-webs & horned burrs
to cling to our legs,
succulent snails cracked underfoot.

An opulence
of gnats & muskrat.


We were 'Gardeners & Astronomers' of that world

—the clangor of the very near, *the sough
of the most remote*—

where bees of cellular savannahs whirred like a summer's day

(humming-birds, within humming-birds)

heard far away.


Where each leaf of every elm
& willow
echoed another realm

of whippoorwill
a world of owl.


And each blue lupine a distant mountain—

& galaxy upon galaxy

of cow-parsley.

\*    \*    \*

'Whatever Natural doth by this Microscope
appear adorned in all imaginable Elegance
and Beauty: such inimitable Gildings and
Embroideries in smallest seeds of Plants:
in parts of Animals, the Head or Eye of a
Fly; Such accurate Order and Symmetry in
the frame of the most minute Creatures, a
Louse or a Mite, as no man were to conceive
without seeing of them. Whereas the most
curious Works of Art seem rude Work as if
they had been done with Mattock or Trowel
so vast a difference is there between the
Skill of Nature and Imperfection of Art.'

\*    \*    \*

'Who placed us with eyes
between a microscopic and a telescopic
world'?

Janáček heard      Ives, in the 5th
squirrels      Symphony,
screeching like his

     wrote the interlapping
clarinet.      counterpoint
And saw night-birds stare      of

into the strings      undulating lines
of his piano.      of mountains
     with

Midges
came from his      celestial

woodwinds

'They have
discovered that several
—even

of the most solid
bodies—
are nothing

but an immense swarm of

imperceptible
Animals'.

'Focus': *fire place.*

326 feet down
in the Moroccan Atlas
French

spelaeologists came upon a

meadow of thick

white gleaming grass.

Leonardo:

'as soon as there
is light,

the air is filled
with innumerable
images

to which the eye serves

orbits

'Whisperings
at a
distance,

correspondence between
darkness and

darkness.

One deep calling
to another'

'Con-sider':
a *gathering of*

*stars.*

Herschel
saw myriad 'worlds
springing up like grass,

in the night'.

The irregular openings
between moving
leaves

of the trees
each
admit a round image

of the sun—
the ground

a shimmer of multiple disks,
except

in eclipse

as a magnet'.


when each forms

Thoreau put his          a crescent.
ear to
the trees
                         Kepler:
'working terribly        'I have touched
within'.                 mountains'.


\*   \*   \*


THE ORBED GARDEN:

Eyebright                *Winged Everlasting*

Globe-thistle                      *Cosmos*

Sunflower           *Aster & Starry Campion*

Aster & Starry Campion        *Sunflower*

Cosmos                      *Globe-thistle*

Winged Everlasting            *Eyebright*


It was here
Thoreau
planted a candle

in the grass,
in a season
the air was so 'inflammable'
it shone 'white and dazzling
and purer and brighter

the farther off it was.


Where earlier—
as reported in that

60

Victorian tome, THE UNIVERSE: *Or,*
                              *The Infinitely Great And*

         *The Infinitely Little*—
                              a Russian
                gentleman,
                              on a whim, transplanted a whole
            avenue of limes

                              upside down, &
                roots
                              were transformed into

            leafy branches.


                              *Light branches, shakes out in leaf.*

      *Darkness puts down roots.*

                              Here, stargrazers
                browse on glowing
                              stubbles
                      among
                              the snail, the thistle-seed
                galaxies.

                              Between the comet's tail
& the 'Horsehead' with dandelion eyes,
                              all is

         pellucid, green, & very shining.


                              *The Eyes At The End*
                *Of The World*—
                              *watching, dilating, inward & outward,*

         *two great stemmed eyes.*


                                                                        61

THE NEXT SOUND YOU HEAR

WILL BE THAT OF TWO GALAXIES,
                              EACH
        THE SIZE OF OUR OWN
                              MILKY WAY,
                  COLLIDING
                              IN SPACE, 500,000 LIGHT YEARS


                  AWAY . . .



                              Centripetal,
                  Centrifugal:

                        *fugue, & petal*

*Songs of the Earth* (1970)

Thoreau, as he walked year after year the Concord woods, was the first to record the musics of silence. "Silence," he writes on his night-walks, "is of various depth and fertility, like soil." "As I leave the village, drawing nearer to the woods, I listen from time to time to hear the hounds of Silence baying the Moon. I hear the unspeakable."

These songs are listenings, as poems must listen and sing simultaneously. They are a progression of hearings of Mahler's "Song of the Earth" on records, in concert, and in my head. In the intervals of the wood thrush singing, and the silence after.

Eartheart hearth is a linkage of ear to hear and heart. Art and hearth are also hid in it. All is at the core of fall. Even the stones here have overtones and the clouds may speak.

These translations and responses might properly be called 'strains'—as in a strain of music or poetry, but also those words & notes which strain their limits outward toward the unutterable.

R.J.

SONGS
OFTHE
EARTH

*twelve squarings of the circle*

earthearthearth
earthearthearth
earthearthearth
earthearthearth
earthearthearth
earthearthearth

```
s tone s
s tone s
s tone s
s tone s

C L O U D
A L O U D
A L O U D
A L O U D
A L O U D
A L O U D
```

*dark behind and*
*dark beyond and*


underneathunder

| | | | | | |
|---|---|---|---|---|---|
| *s* | *p* | *r* | *i* | *n* | *g* |
| *s* | *p* | *r* | *i* | *n* | *g* |
| *s* | *p* | R | I | N | G |
| *s* | *p* | R | I | N | G |
| *s* | *p* | R | I | N | G |
| S | P | R | I | N | G |

be 11 to
11 be 11
to 11 be
11 to 11

wood

wind

```
c     h     o     r          d

      o     o     o
        WOOD
o     o     o     o     o
        WIND
      o     o     o

c     l     o     u     d
```

dark-clouded
spring birds
lark-colored
spring clods
*loud strings*

poem upon poem

form from form
from form from
form from form

open open open

|   | m |   | i |   | n |   | d |
|---|---|---|---|---|---|---|---|
| i |   |   |   |   |   |   | n |
| n |   |   |   |   |   |   | i |
| d |   |   | n |   | i |   | w |

w                                        d

        i                n


        i                n


w                                    g

```
W    A    N    E

     a n e w
W    A    N    E
     a n e w

     a n e w
W    A    N    E
     a n e w

W    A    N    E


        ANEW
        ANEW
        ANEW
        ANEW
```

*world*

*wind*

*f a l l* a l l a l l a

l l *a l l* a l l a l l

a l l *a l l* a l l a l

l a l l *a l l* a l l a

l l a l l *a l l* a l l

and ascend
and ascend
and ascend

to the end




st air st air st air
st air st air st air
st air st air st air
st air st air st air
st air st air st air
st air st air st air

on on on on o
noon on on on
on on on on o
*noon on   noon*

on on on.  .  .

from *Eyes & Objects* (1976)

# WORLD-FRAMED PAGE

molecules on void
6 x 9
(unfinished)

# STILL LIFE

*(Oil on Canvas, c. 1890 by Edwin Romanzo Elmer)*


On the face of it—

it is the-world-as-obsessive-magnifying-glass
set in perpetual balance

in the mouth
of a vast, glass

vase:

from a crystal feather

this polished magnifier (fire)

reflects two windows
once behind us
(the imaginary spectator)

bent by its surface, and inverted.
Invented.

It is the world as Focus,
frame to the lucid

lidless flame.

# STEREOPTICON

*for Lorine Niedecker*

What we wanted

was both words and worlds
you could put your foot through. To be

eye-deep in air,

and the inside of all things
clear

to the horizon. Clear

to the core.

from *RADI    OS* (1977)

# RADI        OS

## O   III

H<sup>AIL</sup>

Bright effluence of bright essence

Whose fountain

                        at the voice

The rising World

Through
                    the Orphean


        descent, and up



To find
                                    the more
Clear
                    song;

Nightly I visit :

Blind

                thoughts that voluntary move
Harmonious numbers



                                summer's rose,




Shine inward, and
                there plant eyes
                            ' that I may see and tell
Of things invisible



                                    once


        thick as stars,


88

The radiant image

                    the only
                    Garden


On the bare outside of this World,




                no bars of Hell, nor




        far off Heaven,

And Man there placed,




                    the sole command,




create




                        or love

from *ARK* (1996)

# BEAM 2

Cloud to ground, the ice electrons move—negative to positive—in stepped bright thrust. Each fifty yard step occurs in less than one one-millionth of a second, the whole zig-zag one to ten yards in luminous diameter. This but corona to a rose-prickle core hotter than the surface of the sun. Positive to negative—the stroke returns gigantic spark, its many-stroked flash a flicker faster than the eye. Every 'point' on this returned jagged channel knocks molecules for miles in links . . .

The circumambient!

in balanced dissent:
enlightenment — on abysm bent.

Angels caged

in what I see,
externity in gauged
antiphony.

(Mid-age. Brought to my knee.)
1935-70

The altitude
unglued

A god in a cloud,

aloud.

Exactitude the flood.

# BEAM 10

*daimon* diamond Monad I
Adam Kadmon in the sky

# BEAM 12

⊙ is the symbol for Sun, the circumference brought to focus at a point. Its outward manifestation is life, just as mind itself seems to unfold some answering chrysanthemum. Beneath a maze pattern on a wall of the church of St. Savino, in Piacenza, the inscription reads: THIS LABYRINTH REVEALS THE STRUCTURE OF THE WORLD. Convoluted of sun and dust, shut dark in a skull, the labyrinth is its own clue. Our lot is puzzlement.

Right auricle, right ventricle, lungs: left auricle, left ventricle, aorta: aorta means 'to lift' or 'heave' and is the great trunk of perception. Branches, from the top of its arch, network the light in our heads — out of a stuff of rays, particles, and pulses: the artificer of reality.

If we represent the three dimensional world we live in as a line, ray, or passage, between the fourth dimension as a globe, then as the universe expands this line describes involutions within that globe. This is the brain of time.

What footprint is left in the snow of flesh by an event? Thinking about thinking moves atoms — however mirrored: and so, as in a rainbow the architecture of light is revealed, mind is a revelation of matter. These wrinkled lobes of flesh, in fact, are more sensitive than the surface of water, and some have watched small eyelids tremble in the womb and wondered could a molecule remember.

The first anatomists likened the brain, pulp and rind, to an orange. Its beginnings are a mulberry of cells, and all desire and despair are seeded in its un- and in-foldings.

Both consciousness and the unconscious 'collect'. It is as if some eons-old mind (in a time when it could do those things) cast the future on its cold eye, saw Plato's cave, and became our brains. Where it will look with us — through "cavernous Earth/Of labyrinthine intricacy, twenty-seven folds of opakeness" — is what you and I are doing this instant. Still, beneath the frontal lobes, at the stem of consciousness, is that reptilian speechless gaze. Man is amphibian to oblivion.

From the ape at my shoulderblade I see angels. Our embryo dreamt the fishes' sleep, became a ripple, leap-frogged itself, and later a mammal: perception is a slingshot drawn back to first plasm.

# BEAMS 21,22,23, *The Song of Orpheus*

O

Tree

into the World,

Man

the chosen

Rose out of Chaos:

Song

*Thunder amid held daffodil,*
*the hills of yellow celandine in sudden sun*
electrum
*'when the light walks'.*


When the light walks, clockwise, counterclockwise,
atoms memorize the firefly's wing
silhouette 20 foot elm leaf
(worm's-eye view through three crisscross timothy stalks).
A blue hinged green at edge, the twilight
sinks as if half swimmer
— ankles in wrinkle through wood turtle
swallowing scarlet strawberry,
waist deep the warp then roof of star split clover, one pale
eye spool rayed Orion
thistle silk through soil particle —
to Euridice. Head deep
in neither
*aether* nether:

"You will find, to the left of The House of *Hades,* a spring . . .

one white leafed cypress at its side".

*"Sometimes the prophet sees the image of Glory*
*in the midst of cloud;*

*but the angel-messenger is invisible*
*because the angelic fire is too pure for one to see.*
*When one sees the fire flaming*
*up from the distance*
*one is only seeing the smoke that*
*surrounds it.*
*Moreover the angel asks:*
What do you see?"

"I have seen the Eternal
*interior,*
*not ocular, vision"*

reply.


PALMS

# B<sub>E</sub>

the man that walk in the way of day and night

like a tree of water, leaf

chaff which the wind

stand in


imagine the earth set against sun,

uttermost parts like a potter's O: trembling sands round about

Arise, and ray.


Stand in

your own heart,

and be still.

the light upon us

in time to the voice of ice:

no throat out in the multitude of ions belled But shout

for joy.

O

save me for

the grave who

all the night make I my bed to swim

.

O

lion, compass

turn

to an end but arrows sing

Out of the mouth of

moon and the stars,

What is man, that made him angels, beasts

to a perpetual end: the gates in the gates of net hid

snared in the turn into sight.

:let them be

imagined.

moved in the secret

ear to hear:

bird to mountain eyelid cup.

They speak tongue tried in a furnace of earth,

on every side,

I sleep the *sleep of*

*all,* not

one.


The lines are fallen to me

in the night seasons.

as the apple of the eye under the shadow of wings,

lion in secret likeness.

voice

shot out lightnings of many waters.

candle:

my steps under me,

consumed.


rose dust before the wind

rock above those that rise up

:man

edge to the world.

sun circuit it: eye in honeycomb heart, hand. name for

ever ever moved

in time the fire shall seed imagined form.


worm shake the womb: I am poured out like water

into the dust of death.

closed unicorn

the ends of the world shall turn

green shadow run.


earth flood into the head

gates; doors; gates; doors; all day enlarged:

an even lace in light and flesh,

the voice of


waters

upon many waters,

The voice of flame shake wild voice from the grave:

down to the remembranch of morning. moved mountain to stand

in my blood, dust dancing:

and ear rock rock out of the spirit hand


out of my mind:

I have heard

My times

lips put to silence; a pavilion of tongues.

cut off from eyes: bones roaring all the day long summer.


in a time when place compass song

I harp an earth full of breath: the sea stood fast.

their works

magnify the exalt together.

matter open wide

clouds like great mountains the fountain of

light shall we see light.


grass-sword heart, time: not again the

seed tree my flesh

before love,

not continually

beauty to consume like a moth: but of the clay,

ears opened from great congregation.


whisper lift

from everlasting to everlasting

meat in praise,

within me: deep call to

deep harp

out arm, and the light

scattered with the forgotten

face,


matter: writer.


though the earth be removed,

*There is*

a river, not moved:

were moved: in the fire.

with the sound of a trumpet wind ends of the round

ear to a parable:

I will open my dark


upon the harp

of compass

inward like the beasts shined before me.

I fold a thousand hills.

I would blood the most High:

frame silence as

self

set in order.


the inward parts: and in the hidden snow walls

the land of a green child is

gone back:

the altogether become one

ion!

the trembling over, a dove at rest

in tempest

:Day and night the midst of it.


thereof: magnify hid changes, words sword the swallow

from falling, light

the shadow lion set on fire, arrow an earth.


I will sing and

Awake my salt to the clouds.

speak to the voice of the great snail sun whirlwind blood

from the run return and go round scatter

the ends of the earth

return up and down.

I will sing

aloud in the morning: to tremble the breaches

of astonishment.

I shall be moved as a bowing wall

delight

in the balance,

every man to his marrow

bend in secret at the perfect fall all flesh come.


waves, and the tumult in uttermost token:

morning and evening

river the year on every side


# Make

a joyful noise

through the flood on foot:

moved as silver net over our heads went fire-shine smoke, Sing

shook snow from the fountain of clouds.

I sink

stranger to prayer

out of the deep waters.

flow me, face to my soul, in my thirst

*let it become*

love turned backward love magnified: wonder lay wait

in the little hills, long moon, mown grass

showers in the dust gold corn

city of the sun all shall call a dream.


ignorant heart: I have put my trust in smoke.


axes upon axes cast fire

in the land.

signs: the borders of turtledove-dissolve: east, west,

full of mixture

ring out, the mountains of sleep.

waking:

The waters saw:

The skies sent out a sound:


thunder path the great know utter our fathers told

us divided

cloud, and all the night with light of

kindled doors

rained down as sand,

the years a wind in hand, locust,

sycamore frost.


the hail flocks to angels fire consumed blood

like water pointed to shine

Turn us again, O

to take deep root, filled with the shadow sent boughs out sea,

branch to the river.

hedge wood and the wild field look down

hand planted with fire,


Turn us again, O

noise to palm, harp psaltery.

Blow the secret place of thunder: wheat

foundations of silence not still, joined like a wheel;

stubble before wind.


flame flesh the sparrownest through; the rain spring out of earth;

voice answer me.

O turn unto her: instrument

I cannot come forth.


The north and the south

in vision alter the thing for ever,

void edge down to the ground how short time is:

What man shall not see death?

footsteps the years past, a sleep: consumed by number

we have seen beauty in the secret place

shadowwings A thousand thousand

eyes in all ways.

against stone I will set sound.


as scattered with oil waves

noise waves things

father the ear, form eye,

thoughts slip the multitude delight

my soul frame

and rock psalm the hills from day to day beauty in beauty

moved:

Clouds trembled.

hills like wax Light is sown in the sight: all ends

Let the floods clap

*between*

the cloudy pillar: singing.


before eyes:

heart cut off perfect

I watch, and

am mad


mingled dust gathered throughout the changed:


frame flower the wind chamber
thunder lace
manifold leviathan play
turn the earth as long as being
face strange another
locus

molten
similitude
joined at the waters ruled east west north south stresses
bands bars waves rings multiplied crease
wake among great answer
cast


compassedless
extend wing in tossed fusion
multitude hand from hand rod midst
willed womb of order strike all a headover wonder
mind forked fast in seed
for ever


light moved for heart fixed
time forth the sun
to behold in out of skip skip turned fountain formed eye
falling toward now as the fire head
us made
Prospero of wand word


hid works
accordion run incline chord law awe accord
harmonies dealt command precept sound
ash consumed settle
I have seen an end of all perfection loves ancient light path
quicken


flesh tremble statue
void above above fine entrance
light standing simple opened order face up river
live
and dawn draw wick to stand as one
great cord

all utter rose rise arrow
eye from foot to sun
going out and coming in from
time
compact of seed
file stream


I dream
the sheaves sleep quiver speak in furrow
to the mower by the depths
I wait and watch for the morning from all eyes
matter as swarm clothed with vision
each bud a lamp


the head stand in lightning
wind out of throughout for ever for ever for ever alone
out the water great lights stretched out
divided into parts through the midst ever flesh
rivers of willowsong
against stone


magnified far off I walk
compass behind and before take wing about me
the dark and the light both alike
I awake
and know my heart
the way exalt


scattered

I looked on the land of the living

as those that have been long dead within within me

I stretch forth the morning

a song of ten strings

I will sing to all will hear their being

stars infinite

swift snow before wind suns flying

into a twoedged firmament

sounding

*Eden* (handwritten)

# BEAM 30, THE GARDEN

Center (handwritten)

man ; center / has cancer (handwritten)
of molecule / radiation patient (handwritten)
for Patricia Anderson

"To do as Adam did"

through the twilight's fluoride glare Mercury in perihelion

(rotating exactly three times

while circling the sun twice)

to Pluto foot tilt up the slide at either plane

and build a Garden of the brain.


Internetted eternities, interspersed

with cypresses

ply ringed air about the many spectacled apples there.

Flamestitch niches orb in swivel orb, The Muses thrush at center

turning. *Phospheros arborescens* they sing

sense's


struck crystal clarities

to knock the knees

(or scarlet hollyhock, against a near blue sky).

No end of fountains lost among the shrubberies full eye may bare.

Fixed stars

with fireflies jam the lilac.

Adam - center of creation & energy of God (handwritten)
Atom - center of molecule (handwritten)

The Lord is a delicate hammerer.

Gold hive upon gray matter

He taps synapse ("carrying to") ("carrying away")

an immense bronze pinecone moon-knit at the end of a vista

of sunny *jets d'eau,* silver poplars. All

shivered in a pool.


Literally, a flowing: form-take-hand

-with-form

(That Which Fasteneth Us)

pillar to pillar the great dance arch itself through all that

is or was or will be, 3/4 time. This will be a glade

at the head of one stream


and a resonant gnomon before it will stretch regions of signaling

gnat-like resiliencies in the atmosphere

of where we are —

or were.

Or will be, when the mingled frame of mind

of man is celebration.

almost set in kansas
writing about familiar
* naive artist

Gates, which separate the wings

of tiered ilex, open

in caverns of atoms passing from one into another's zenith

of periodic movement, vast helicoidal shift:

a vaulting of arteries

beating their heads against the dark.


This is the body of light.

Vertically in a chromatic spread chord

— Elysian elision —

*J'avais bâti, dans un rêve, un palais, un château ou des*

*grottes*

along the lines of sight.

Dear Garden:


This is the way the world begins, the word begins.

Through here,

where grow the galax and aster together,

I have planted Shadow illuminating The Field of Glittering

Opposites:

*ange arc-en-ciel*


*flocons de neige*

I have attempted a temple as if hierarchies of music

beating against time gone adagio, that is the Secret Pool we return

to. And not to stone

but to the world behind its human

mirror.

This is the way the word begins, the world begins,

wrestling the old ineffable to Bosch's amazing white giraffe

— or St. Rousseau

intent a symmetry of whisker.

Love itself is a kind of *mirage* nesting it all

together. Around a center


no one can see the end of at the Well of The Bottomless,

I have placed parallels of bright guardians

"along with the trill

of the Nightingale,

and the call of the European quail"

as in The Pastoral.


(Signed) *THE GARDENER*


P.S.


"I have refracted it with Prismes, and reflected with it Bodies which in Day-light were of other colours; I have intercepted it with the coloured film of Air interceding two compressed plates of glass; transmitted it through coloured Mediums, and through Mediums irradiated with other sorts of Rays, and diversly terminated it; and yet could never produce any new colour out of it. But the most surprising, and wonderful composition was that

Newton

of *Whiteness*."

is this happening,
a quick as a squirrel's tail
spright of deer
but burnished as a
grackle
foci
evenly distributed as nesting sights
or silvery layers of film
over rotifers
trapeze
of paraphrase
in a sphere clumped
pool all a mareshiver
of lights
executed in pure
katydid
half Mozart
fits and starts, half stars
both
holywork of oracular oak
thought through
dust's
simplest
scherzo scarecrow
tactics an acorn might
knuckle under
paradise
and pairs of eyes
past
all believing

an edifice
of matched snailshell
faced to watch
Bach
in cherubim cliffed hayseed, rayed
cloud in plaster
forever
or near it
as consonance gets without
clef
to unraveled blizzard
huzzah cooperating with treble instances
such as orioles
between tulip trees
seizing the summerier dissonances
of worm
bees purring a
cappella
in utter emerald cornfield
till the cows come
purple home
this is paradise
this is
happening
on the surface of a bubble
time and again
fire sculpt of notwithstanding
dark
the whole parted world
in choir

when the wind's bright horses
hooves break earth in thunder
that,
that is paradise
Lord Hades, whom we all will meet
crackling up
like a wall of prairie fire
in a somersault silver
to climb blank air
around us
to say then head wedded nail and hammer to the
work of vision
of the word
at hand
that is paradise
this is called spine of white cypress
roughly cylindrical
based
on the principle
of the intervals between cuckoos
and molecules, and molecules
reechoing:
these are the carpets of
protoplast, this
the hall of crystcycling waltz
down carbon atom
this, red clay
grassland
where the cloud steeds clatter out wide stars
this is

# ARK 58, *Balloon on Being 50*

(by letter)

Keats to Shelley —

"load every rift with ore"

Zuk to RJ: "'S Okay!"

Advise Chas O: "Steal the stuff"

& me to me

*sail we manmade reservoir:*

revise, surprise,

suppose


a r o u n d  a  y e a r

t o d a y  I  s o u n d

f u t u r e  a  f a c e

r a f t e r  o f  a i r

h e a r t ' s  f e a t s

f o u n d  e d i f i c e

of pyramids, a
myriad afire

set out to swallow dark
in a nutshell,

back in the Garden
no Fall before

self left
asway fate's work

"sun cut off
at the neck"

Apollinaire!
Apollinaire!

\*

gear aerie
the real article
heaven fled to ledge

limb unsealed from limb
for wings'
alert machinery

& wield a torch
as sphere
held arch of time

transfigured moat
grasp ear
in chalice host

*

rhyme twine
mirror rim mirror
to remind mired any mortal
stiles arrayed,
choir
prise air

# ARK 63, *BUILDER'S SPIRE*

On the road to Samarkand, to Xanadu
Sam Palmer's
"little dells, nooks, corners of Paradise"
tented with light
(deep in the Antipodes
fix identity)
straightway every jot & tittle
count like a bell
rung out bold under hammer!

Blazing casements,
electron a-chisle stuff
of thistle, stook of hay against set sun
& every edgehog spark out day.
Noman ribbed anew red clay, figurehead prairie
to walk abroad
ripped lightning thru oncoming dusk
miles from nowhere
till the moon swallow sky.

Carousel, lid to world,
ends arm in arm
liver & lights on cue summon pulse, us
weld cataract a seat such bronc
as attic rooster
with escape hatch (steepled) crow.
Plains dawn a ramparts dimmed in just & golden maji.
Seek humanity dogged
in the footsteps of Sphinx

alive anew, alike unique.
There Orpheus ask up Euridice —
of winter tumbleweed
all summer unleashed upon one goldenrod
to naked eye,
earth air water, afire
'faire dandylion'
maybe monkeywrench a millionth untold tangible
— but beauty bare,

green grass writ Sanskrit
to worm below as well hawk a speck beyond cerulean.
All stone to flute aspire
('Thunder & Blazes' on calliope)
to speed the race
sez Old Hocus-Pocus
above round of moon and new under the sun,
twice the height snail cosmos
lantern become:

torch held ceiling cave
in charcoal, ochre, sinew scrawl
forebears' "you must change"
(thereby in target, might distant stars abound
attained delight)
doors opened through thrones of space
— each cell a panoply
thumb of time —
seated center many a bubble.

# ARK 65, *Windmill Spire*

s t a r b o a r d
b o t h  s o u n d  u s
c e l e s t i a l  i n c i d e n t,
a n c e s t r a l  d a n c e
n e w c l e a r:


up to now

escutcheon noon

Noah, Ezekiel — noun & verb

slacking and fastening

slap-dash past's

*non pareil*

untold stories deep

'drawing room'

stripped not incidentally of identities

to crack the puzzle

(an unexplained

oneness, ornateness)

truckle we mortal

quest all edged existence ask

here, rhyme may be

anywheres

stubborn timber

splinter off the very orb

our fabric itself

*light raiment*

a pattern of rafters'

it is it was it will be opt

tho browsprit Night,

'dome's day'
mount perennial herald!
4 winds in the shape of beasts bucking tide
whisker the Complete Combine Harvester
in every tumbleweed
caught wind to barbed-wire:
Kansas Aweigh
keel manifold, sped bones in colloquy steep wheatear
Land Diver
bound round the world
dawn bandshell
no bright deed remembered laid to rest

loam wherein held we steady sail
who fold our dust close
sparest of forms
resurrect an Ararat
ever recarved
of the visible curved universe —
for if hell indeed rein time stood still
and paradise thus daily fall
unlikely wings
on usual shoulders,
scrawl on my stone *bois d'arc* pulled off Great Plains
*tour d'borizon*
— Pegasus every point maximum surface —
(our Osage Orange, called so from the Indian's bows)

ATTEMPTED THIS LADDER FOR ST. JACOB
ASTRADDLE BOTTOMLESS WELL
R. J. FECIT

"" And he lighted upon a certain
place, and tarried there all night,
because the sun was set; and he
took of the stones of that place,
and put *them* for his pillows, and
lay down in that place to sleep."

# ARK 70, ARCHES IV

on the plains' road
to the tower
pray hold flourish rainbow lyre

who fell or flew at will,
a spring there holds the Deluge
athroat rock

"placed in the luminous air"
full arch a sky
hack path out to sea

head beyond horizon's
inside bend to
vanish lock & key, illustrious

in large measure
seated (by the by) in flame
ever in another sphere

wondering where swim I am's,
zenith Kansas
vs. eternal city

in furnace of seeming
free mind, hurled athwart world
once Kingdom come

if step aboard
eyes, language of flight
(every space borne inspection)

every shape reply to a force,
here where we were
seismic avenues aligned

taken wing, time being
a dream of stone
hinge wedge lever incline pulley

to build a temple there
without floor, roof candle bed
mind into window

spit image, means to some end
in echelon ion
where ladder = knuckle

why knot thus: so as
upon a time once phoenix in fact
halcyon elude hatchet

"in this yard
— you could break your neck
looking at a star"

trained choir, inlaid semblage
proof beyond wed soul
mankind undamned

built literally out the dark,
Walled Demesne
cut enigmatic figure

Stonehenge, marble core of moon
by tall winds sawed
long ago planted far field

cave cut behind waterfall,
gift blind life
bud multiple new eye

# ARK 74, ARCHES VIII (FROM THOREAU'S JOURNALS)

"and something more I saw
left off understanding, around bend
encircling world

Words lie like boulders on a page
woods black as clouds,
blood durable as aqueduct

no surface bare long —
earth covered deep alphabet
this spring laid open with my hoe,

down stream, eyes levelled at you
assume a true sphericity
and bay the moon

multiply deeds within, a cynosure
that every star might fall
into its proper place

being, the great explainer
as if the earth spoke
and heavens crumpled into time

vast glow-worm in fields of ether
as if answered its end,
tail curled about your vitals

sea of mowing, seeing no bottom
leaves ply and flowing fill up path
and thunder near at hand

like summer days seen far away
golden comb, successive lines of haze
set fire to the edges

a crow's wing in every direction,
very deep in the sod
bursting a myriad barrier

as if a cavern unroofed
this great see-saw of brilliants,
oclock strikes whippoorwill

swayed as one, from I know not what
see stars reflected
in the bottom of our boat

chandeliers of darkness
I saw sun shining into like depths,
both planet and the stubble

within compass of a spark
the flute I now hear
on pinnacle, to the end of days

Wing horse, the veery trill
go about search echo
mountains already left these shores

I look under the lids of time,
left without asylum
to gather a new measure

through aisles of ages
art, every stroke of the chisel
enter own flesh and bone

without moving a finger;
turning my very brain
reflected from the grass blades"

# ARK 77, ARCHES XI

steeped in makeshift
"one that loved the sun,
and sent its root down deep"

bare record of the word
umbilical, a fellow carpentree
stand but in my head

too much, too soon, fast epitaph
Opus Twin Opposites
helix matter in own right

medallion of spun glass,
sentience itself testament as
ability toll bell

earth spinning its axis
two veins & artery
counterclockwise brain's coil

rib of white whale
to tail pulled blue-eyed lion,
in the middle of nowhere

astride one great divisible,
*aurora borealis*
thru backward of time

mute, numinous
set to number how many streaks
on each curl of a tulip

swimming upstream to Messiah
hook line & sinker
arrest in crystal, flow

the wine-dark sea
any Odysseus order as wave,
if snail crawl equal lightspeed

where beast, rare
upon Isle of the Blest reside
shrouded in accuracy

behold stage to stage,
the curtain held
to last pounce intelligence

revolve about one one's body
almost above notice,
while soul practice nail

any stretch of imagination —
to rise and cry out
like putty in your hands

breezes, Hesperides
feats under great spread wisdome
to speed the day, mold clay

pitchfork the un-sea-sing
and moon stupa sun,
leverage veritable deepenings

actXity sunder brainstem,
storm in the head
countour everything believable

"fraction wave through fraction,
reaction solve reaction"
inVerse salvation

# ARK 91, *Arches XXV*

Off top of my head
seed, honeycomb, vine curl,
shells, snake on branch

mind in orderly array —
forms molded trial & error
living out suitcase

the tide and toll of time
plus pull of space,
*snowstorms by starlight*

*a landscape of Simulars,*
*where shape sort inked shape*
old as the hills

lept dolphin-wise,
plow many psyched that sea
absolutely unbottomed

balance the raftered known
so knock The Messenger,
*a door open on*

so steady a prestidigitation,
any scene summoned
swirled forth first core

each one faster than the last,
angels upon ladders
vanish Archimboldo elms

wild card shot human deck:
Maypole of image
& compass indissoluable

to oar the Uproar!
yet cross to bear, row to hoe
hollering down town well

knock in the dark
*the key to the horizon, yours* —
*don't lock up behind*

yet only by secret handshake
under the Mallorn trees,
and get out fast

(a roll far thunder)
furrow albeit ready ground —
Seasons taken for a ride

gallop, wrapped the world
bold Aurora Borealis
all in an opening of a drawer

"these trees will be my books"
*over my dead leaves* . . .
hide how we can

face of the deep,
stars through unmeasured
heights of pendant atmosphere

only winged imagination
cement horsesense,
no fall of an apple unforseen

Unfolding worlds before us,
atom become unto flesh
branched pitchfork

# ARK 96, ARCHES XXX

*[handwritten annotation: bricks— individual parts to make a whole]*

*[handwritten annotation: each word holds so much meaning in itself]*

"The silver light
turned every blade of grass,
every particle of sand

into a luminous
metallic splendor; there was
nothing however small

that did not clash
in the bright wind, that
did not send

arrows of light
through the glassy air"
wrote Ansel Adams!

All night, at golden hive
busiest of Being
lustrous intelligence

cast throughout darkness,
tackling the eternal
bluest guitar — *[handwritten annotation: Picasso]*

set against Time
roll back yr mortal lids,
sentry of statuary

*[handwritten annotation: Spiritual epiphany]*

innumerable numinosities
mind set ajar;
thru wildering gyre

throat aloft, afloat —
truths to the World's edge
grace amazing tell

outside the door
red wheelbarrow glint rain,
Anyone might see it

let up the blinds
as sap mount into tree,
scribed lark in jubilation

magnetic, torch antiphony
tail universe end/on
waltz seasons all four

death sweet be not yet,
I tread the stars
in perilous anatomy

over bottomless pit
only intricater;
I thread evolving Heaven

"nequamquam vacuum"
flamestitch I symmetries:
weaver oriole's nest

I construct ahive
suns one can't gaze upon
surpassing foresight,

*only Hand with Language*
nothing unknowable
fate, the Undoer

home everlasting
(memory, tenacious anemone)
await composer Sword

from *The Shrubberies*
(previously unpublished)

quincunx of succulents

subtle colors and forms

succinct in dust


appropriate the pot

assigned, set each

for spill into Other


always my core dream

winding a garden

secret in every sense

Yes Heaven/being/garden

create, destroy, to be

through noxious fumes

lava scarlet flow

sunder, sunder, sunder

part foliage to see
the Goddess triumphant
recumbent Hercules

Zeus, Jesus, jeeses
on breeze, cicadas
swallowing the sword

sun in the honeyhives
combing order from time,

light on light suffuse
like liquid copper

climbing in the dark
ore heights Byzantine

# A Step Nearer

an expanse of lawn
situated with robins

listening to worm
wear way through roots

stance alert upright
and all in silence

Presence only, disturb
then dip in flight

blast dandelion-seed
but perch freedom won

# SIDE LIGHT

billions mistakes
amoebe into man

jammed sky the while
stark labyrinth

seethed with flesh
with ache seized

stroke unlimited amethyst

pencil in exact bumblebees,

among bronze lacquer cacti

so rampart senses incensed

lift sentient to the skies

again and again and again

westward into darkness

in realms of whippoorwill

yet glinting off leaves

in the Forest of Arden

From here, across the Mts.

everything is quite different

customs, architecture, smell

but same appetite for Hell

every year there is

The Night of Fireflies

rising, rising to

bower of the infinite

a room of dried lavender

cupboards of euphoria

shield acres of tobacco

just ripe to be picked

# Last Poem

shambles this way

antipodean being

come full circle

sparks in darkness

lightning'd eternal return

flipped the ecliptic

Designed by
Samuel Retsov

Text: 11 pt Minion
Titles: 16 pt Minion Display

acid-free paper

Printed by
McNaughton & Gunn